Promoting Your Union

Six strategies to get more organizing leads and union members

BY
Jason Mann

Acknowledgements

From the outset this book has been a co-operative effort. It could not have happened without the organizing directors and field organizers who participated in the surveys and interviews that led to this book.

I'd also like to thank everyone who provided feedback and advice including Javier Ybarra, Greg Garratt, Carol Fehner, Maura Lane, Joe Orawczyk, Dennis Fallen, Bruce Scherer, Diane Ersbo, James Nichols, Bob Oedy, Patrick Johnson, Louis Watanabe, Mark Horn, Scott Eickholt, Erik Forman, Lynn Woods, Andy Griggs, Rebekah David, Scott Eickholt, Ken Little, Loren Crawford, Robert Martinez, Alex White, Adam Knobel, Leanne Shingles, Jody Jones, Tim Dymond, Keith Hodgson.

Also a special thanks to Jim Sinclair, Jef Keighley, Jarrah Hodge and Frank Pozzobon for going beyond with your support and feedback.

To get free training videos
on four of the best ideas
from this book visit

www.PromotingYourUnion.com

Table of Contents

Introduction

Fundamentals
Chapter 1
Setting Organizing Targets that Encourage Growth   5
Chapter 2
Communicating the Union Advantage   14
Chapter 3
Measuring Your Outreach Efforts   22

Promotion Strategies
Chapter 4
Creating an Online Lead Generation Machine   29
Chapter 5
*Getting Organizing Leads at Strategic Targets Through
Agitation/Education Campaigns*   50
Chapter 6
The 10,000 Prospect Strategy   58
Chapter 7
Using Facebook to Get Organizing Leads   74
Chapter 8
*Building a Relationship with Workers Before They Enter
the Workforce*   90
Chapter 9
Engaging Union Members in Organizing   95

Appendix
A Quick-Start Guide to Getting More Organizing Leads   105

Introduction

This is a book to help union organizers get more organizing leads, create outreach plans to bring in new members and build the power of their unions.

It's based on conversations with organizers and outreach plans that unions have successfully used to expand their organizing.

I had a conversation with another organizer a few months ago who told me, "It is impossible to organize right now. The system is stacked against working people. The smartest thing we can do is just wait until we get card check or better organizing laws."

I've never agreed with this approach. Despite restrictive labour laws, there are unions organizing successfully and growing in an environment without card check.

If we use look at what they are doing differently, we can find ways to organize in spite of the challenges.

It doesn't mean that we shouldn't work to make joining a union a right rather than a risk – just that we can't say it is impossible to organize in this environment while some unions are having organizing success.

In talking with many union organizers I've found that the unions that are growing don't leave it to chance. They generally have some type of outreach strategy to get new leads and quality campaigns.

There are many academic books on union organizing and a few books on tactics to win union elections. However there isn't much on creating an outreach plan to promote your union to non-union workers.

Ultimately union organizing isn't about signing cards - it's about empowering people and changing lives. It's about building power and improving conditions for working people as a whole.

We can't do this reaching 30 people at a time - shop by shop. We need to create plans to reach thousands of workers.

The first three chapters of this book look at the foundations of creating an outreach plan: targeting, communications and measuring impact.

The remaining chapters contain six strategies that unions are using to reach non-union workers on a mass scale.

The ideas in this book aren't based on what might work - or abstract models of trade unionism - but actual best practices from union organizers who are using these tactics in the field.

Chapter 1: Setting Organizing Targets that Encourage Growth

Chapter 1 looks at how to set targets in your outreach plan so that your organizing wins build on each other. It will show you the 5 criteria to consider when creating a targeting strategy.

Chapter 2: Communicating the Union Advantage

Chapter 2 sets out how to create a core outreach message for non-union workers and how to talk with the type of person likely to contact a union.

Chapter 3: Measuring Your Outreach Efforts

Chapter 3 examines how to measure and track your outreach efforts to find out what is working and find areas where you have opportunities for growth.

Chapter 4: Creating an Online Lead Generating Machine

More non-union workers view your union's join page than read your leaflets or speak to your organizers. Union organizers need to fundamentally change how they use the Internet. Chapter 4 shows how to create an organizing website that is effective at generating leads.

Chapter 5: The Agitation / Education Campaign

Agitation/education campaigns are long-term campaigns that will help you keep in touch with workers at strategic targets without leaving burnt turf from failed drives.

Chapter 6: The 10,000 Prospect Strategy

The 10,000 prospect strategy is a campaign to build up a large contact database of non-union workers in your sector, build a relationship with these workers and then turn the contacts into organizing leads.

Chapter 7: Using Facebook for Union Organizing

While many unions have experimented using social media, most haven't succeeded in getting the number of leads they would like. Chapter 7 looks at how to use Facebook to help get organizing leads for your union.

Chapter 8: Reaching Workers Before They Enter the Workforce

By investing early we can build a relationship with workers in our industry before they enter the workforce.

Chapter 9: Getting Organizing Leads from Members

Engaging members in organizing and building a culture of organizing are critical to building union density. Chapter 9 covers your organizing department's biggest asset – your union's members.

Chapter 1: Setting Organizing Targets that Encourage Growth

The Virtuous Organizing Cycle

Unions that succeed at organizing have a targeting strategy where one organizing victory builds upon and leads to another.

The Virtuous Cycle

- Effective targeting builds power and power increases your leverage.

- Increasing your leverage allows you to negotiate stronger contracts and better serve your members.

- Better contracts, better service to your members and more power means more resources can be freed up for organizing.

Relying on hot shops for organizing leads creates a vicious cycle where organizing new units ultimately will lead to fewer members organized.

- New units that don't strengthen or build upon your power require more resources to service.

- The resources come out of servicing industries where you do have power.

- Reduced power and fewer resources available means fewer resources for organizing.

Organizing Outreach Plans Need Specific Targets

Who exactly is your union trying to attract and who are you not trying to attract?

Targeting is a critical element of any outreach plan because it allows your union to focus its limited resources on areas where you'll make the biggest gains in members and power.

Setting priorities and organizing targets is necessary so that organizers spend their time only on targets that are the best fit for your union.

Five Criteria for a Targeting Strategy

1. Power - Will this target strategy grow your union's power?

- Where do you currently have bargaining power?
- Would you gain bargaining power at other units by organizing this one?
- Is the employer province wide or country wide?

- Is the employer profitable?

- With focused effort, could you sign up enough employees to have an impact?

- Would organizing this target industry or employer increase your union's power or decrease its power by spreading its resources too thin?

2. Footholds - Will this targeting strategy grow your footholds?

Look at units where you represent only a fraction of a workforce. Your footholds in an industry are either growing or dying. If you aren't organizing areas where you have footholds, they will eventually decertify.

Make a decision to lean into areas where you have footholds and make a serious attempt to organize or be content to let your footholds leave slowly over time.

Either decision is fine but rather than dabbling, decide.

3. Your Membership - Will this target strategy excite and mobilize your membership?

- How will organizing this target affect support for an organizing program within your union?

- Will members volunteer to help organize this target?

Picking targets that excite your membership helps create a culture of organizing.

4. Non-Union Workers- What is the impact on non-union workers in the industry as a whole?

- What is the larger impact if you organized this employer or industry?
- Would it lead to future organizing victories?
- Would it spark a conversation at other non-union worksites?

Organizing the auto industry in the United States sparked a wave of industrial organizing. What is the equivalent in your sector?

5. Winnable - Is the campaign winnable?

Historically the labour movement's biggest organizing victories have come from sectors that everyone said were impossible to organize. That being said - make sure your local has the take on to organize the targets you set out for yourself.

Strategic Long-Term Targets

Strategic campaigns are special targets that have the potential to build the greatest amount of power for your union.

They also tend to be the hardest to organize.

These are targets you could work on for years without success and then suddenly have significant results.

With strategic campaigns it is important to take action every single day to stay top of mind with the workers.

You might consider setting up separate websites, specific material or separate organizing teams for these targets.

How to Select Strategic Targets

Many organizers have told me that a good way to determine strategic targets is to make a list of <u>all possible targets</u> you could organize in a sector and rank them using the five factors I've set out above.

The industries or employers that land in the top two positions are likely the best strategic targets for your union.

The Trap of Strategic Targets

There is much to do in the labour movement. Too many good projects. Too many important things. Too many good targets.

Some unions make the mistake of have too many strategic targets. Having 10 or 20 strategic targets is the same as having no priorities.

At most aim to have two or three strategic targets depending on your sector.

Beggars Can't Be Choosers

I went to Ontario to speak with an organizer of a small local to discuss strategies to grow the union where he worked.

After suggesting he create a target strategy and refuse to organize leads that are not on his target list he said to me:

"Turning away organizing leads might make sense if we had more leads than we knew what to do with," he said, "but at this point if someone comes to us and wants to join our union - we need to take any members we can get."

I suggested he take a look at unions that are having organizing success and divide the size of their budget by the number of members they are organizing.

On average they are spending around $1,000 for every member they successfully bring into the union.

Considering even the most successful unions spend $1,000 for every new member they organize - chasing hot shops - just because a single person approaches you about joining - means you'll never be in a position where one organizing victory builds upon another.

How Can We Turn Down Someone Who Wants to Join a Union?

A common objection to a prioritized approach to targeting goes something like this:

"If there are workers who want to organize, how can we morally say no to someone who needs our help?"

There's no doubt that every worker should have a union at their workplace

But that's not really the issue.

We need to figure out as a labour movement:

- How do we organize the largest section of the working class in the shortest possible time?
- How can we use our limited resources most effectively?
- How can we organize key industries that build power of the labour movement as a whole?

We can't accomplish any of these things without a strategic approach to targeting.

If someone isn't a good fit for your union refer him or her to another union that can help.

Chasing hot shops to get a few new members in the short run will ultimately reduce the number of workers you will be able to organize in the long run.

The Benefits of Having a Clear Target List

For union members:

Setting out who you are looking to organize (and who you aren't interested in organizing) helps members talk to their friends and refer organizing leads to you.

For servicing staff:

Clear targeting helps create conversation on the shop floor.

Asking, "Do you know anyone who works a Comcast?" will start more conversations than, "You wouldn't know anyone who wants to join a union would you?"

For field organizers:

Setting targets helps organizers build knowledge for a particular employer or industry.

Building up 50 contacts in three industries is more valuable than 100 contacts spread over 15 industries.

Action Exercise: Setting Organizing Targets that Encourage Growth

1. Create a list of targets looking at the criteria of bargaining power, footholds, impact on membership, impact on the non-union sector, and winnable campaigns.

2. Pick two to three strategic targets by ranking all of your targets and picking the targets at the top of the list that would have the biggest long-term impact on your union if organized.

3. Resolve not to go after any industry or employer not

covered by your target list.

Chapter 2: Communicating the Union Advantage

How We Talk About Unions Makes a Difference

Given that workers who unite in unions are better off than those who do not – why isn't everyone a union member?

The problem your union faces isn't creating advantages for being a union member – it's communicating the advantages of being part of your union.

Are There Other Obstacles?

Of course there are. Big ones.

Suggesting that the only limiting factor is communicating our message would be to underestimate the obstacles workers face from employers.

We know the super rich spend millions of dollars each year to interfere with workers' democratic right to join unions.

We know that the 1% spend millions helping elect governments that advocate stripping workers' rights to join unions.

We know that big business spends millions on think tanks, foundations and research grants to shift public discourse on the trade-union movement and progressive politics.

We know that employers set up a legal system which is stacked against workers and the ability to organize.

However, all these are objective factors that we can't do anything to change in the short term without a fundamental change to the system.

To unite working people to fight for change we need to get better at organizing.

Communicating Our Values

Kate Bronfenbrenner and Robert Hickey wrote a brilliant article - "Winning is Possible: Successful Union Organizing in the United States — Clear Lessons, Too Few Examples" - which uncovered a secret of successful union organizing campaigns that's worth mentioning.

Certain messages appeared in successful organizing drives that did not appear in unsuccessful campaigns.

The researchers discovered that organizing drives that focused on values like respect, fairness, dignity, justice and a voice at work were more successful than campaigns that focused on grievance procedures, wage increases, or individual workplace problems.

When we share the values at the heart of our movement, we will find and attract other workers who share our values.

No Cookie-Cutter Approach

Your task is to create an outreach message that speaks to values and resonates with workers in the industry you are organizing.

It will vary from sector to sector. You'll have to dig deep based on whom you are looking to organize.

How to Find Underlying Themes

While working with an IBEW local we came up with an exercise to create a profile of the type of worker who calls a union.

We listed of every individual who had contacted them in the last five years and considered:

- What did these people have in common?
- What stories did they share?
- What had they tried at work before contacting the union?
- What were their demographics?
- What were their attitudes?

Targeting the "Joiners"

Your main outreach message should be directed at the "joiner" – the type of person at a workplace who contacts a union.

You will get more leads this way than if you tried to convincing workers that aren't the type to call a union office.

When you write your organizing leaflets, advertisements or webpage material, you should picture yourself talking to a person who fits this "joiner" personally.

Dig Deeper on the "Joiner"

- What do they aspire to?
- What do they fear? What are they afraid is going to happen?
- How do they view themselves?
- How do they see the world?
- What is the story of their life?

Why Workers Contact Unions

No one joins your union because it was founded 100 years ago.

When talking to potential members, many organizers make the mistake of speaking to why they feel workers should join a union as opposed to why workers do join unions.

Tapping into Deeper Emotions of the Joiner

The reasons why someone approaches you about joining a union are usually emotional.

Talking on an emotional level is the difference between saying:

"Join our union because unionized employees make on average 30% more than other workers"

vs.

"You work hard for a living and should be able to make ends meet at the end of the month."

"Get paid more – become a union electrician"

vs.

"Electricians are in demand – shouldn't you get paid what you're worth?"

"The company made $2.3 million dollars in the last year - they should provide a three-per-cent wage increase"

vs.

"Your hard work makes the company successful, it's only fair that you should be paid fairly for the work you do."

Speak About the Prospective Member - Not Yourself

Frame your union's core outreach message around what is in it for the prospective member reading the message.

Don't say: "We have a staff of experienced professionals."

Experienced staff isn't a reason to join your union - it's a minimum expectation.

Say:

"Joining a union means you have knowledgeable advocates on your side when speaking with management"

Rather than

"Our union has 30 servicing representatives with years of experience"

Why Did Workers Join Your Union in the Past?

Exit surveys can provide insight on how to talk about your union with prospective members.

I worked with an SEIU local to setup an exit survey system for their organizing department.

What we discovered is how much a worker made per hour had little impact on if they wanted to join a union.

Someone who made $9/hr. was as likely to want to join a union as someone who made $14/hr.

The exit surveys revealed that what really mattered was "relative pay" – how a worker's pay compared to their conception of fairness.

The local confirmed what many organizers have long suspected, leaflets that talk about "getting paid more" won't be as successfully as leaflets that talk about "being paid fairly for the work you do."

When you have an unsuccessful campaign do an exit survey with that group to find out what went wrong.

When you have a successful campaign do an exit survey to find out what went right.

- How did people perceive your union?
- Why did people sign a card?

Action Exercise: Communicating the Union Advantage

1. Create a list of everyone who contacted your union about joining in the past five years.

2. Identify the "joiner" profile for your union. What are the demographics? What do the people who contact you about joining have in common? Create a picture of what this "joiner" looks like.

3. Write down the urgent needs and compelling desires of people who want to join your union.

4. Review your organizing materials to ensure they speak to the type of person who contacts a union rather than workers

in general.

5. Start conducting exit surveys on campaigns to find out how to better communicate your outreach message to prospective members.

To watch an online video on how to communicate to non-union workers go to http://www.PromotingYourUnion.com

Chapter 3: Measuring Your Outreach Efforts

What Are You Measuring?

Most unions have organizing goals and generally have an idea of what success looks like based on a certain number of workers or workplaces organized.

Are You Measuring Your Outreach Efforts?

- How are you tracking the activities you take every day to make your phone ring?
- How are you measuring outreach success?
- Have you found ways to measure the effectiveness of different outreach methods?

The Power of Lead Goals and Benchmarking

Setting specific benchmarks for getting leads in your outreach plan allows you to focus your effort on what is working.

It allows you to see into the future to determine whether you are on track with your organizing goals.

Measuring your outreach efforts allows you to make course corrections if your outreach plan isn't working so you can redirect resources.

The Union Organizing Funnel

Picture the organizing process as a funnel.

At the top of the funnel are workers researching joining a union.

Of that group, a number will contact you about joining and smaller number will actually meet with you.

Eventually, an even smaller number will form an inside committee.

An even smaller number will turn into campaigns and a smaller number again will get to a vote.

Finally, of that group a smaller number will vote yes.

Visualizing organizing as a funnel shows you where to improve in the organizing process.

I visited a local once that in a year had 80 organizing leads, four active campaigns and two wins.

Because they measured their outreach effort they knew the way to organize more workers wasn't to get better at winning elections, or getting better at house calls, but converting organizing leads into campaigns.

However if the union had 80 leads, 40 active campaigns, 10 votes and 5 wins, the numbers would suggest a need to put more time into improve card signing and getting to a vote.

If your union only tracks "wins" or "members organized," you'll have no idea where to start working on making your organizing department more effective.

How to Set Lead Generation Goals

The easy way to determine organizing lead benchmarks is to work backwards from your union's organizing goals.

If you know the percentage of leads that turn into campaigns, the percentage of campaigns that get to a vote and the percentage of elections that the union wins - you can use those figures to determine your lead generation benchmarks.

For example, if half your organizing leads turn into campaigns, half those campaigns get to a vote and half those votes result in a win, your success rate is about 12%.

($\frac{1}{2}$ x $\frac{1}{2}$ x $\frac{1}{2}$ = 1/8 or 12%)

The law of probability suggests you would need eight organizing leads for every successful campaign.

Why Not Just Track Wins?

Organizers should spend their time face to face with workers, not staring at an Excel spreadsheet.

But there are reasons you may want to consider tracking organizing leads.

- You can see if you are on track and make course corrections.
- It allows you to track the performance of individual organizers assigned to generating organizing leads.
- It identifies areas in the organizing process where you have room to improve.

Shots on Goal

Why do hockey teams track shots on goal and goals scored rather than just the number of games the team has won?

Sometimes your organizing team will not succeed at organizing a workplace because of external factors beyond their control.

However, it's also true that your organizing team will sometimes lose campaigns that they should have won.

That's why it's important to have other metrics like organizing leads generated to measure the success of your organizing team.

Even the best hockey team won't win every game.

Sometimes things don't go their way. Maybe a bad call – a lucky goal or an unfortunate penalty will impact the outcome of the game.

However, if the team barely took any shots on goal the coach knows there is a problem.

Measure What Matters

Here's what you should be measuring regularly:

1. Active Campaigns

   These are campaigns with a reasonable chance of getting to a vote. If the number of active campaigns is low - move more resources into lead generation.

2. Prospect List Size

   These are people who have contacted your union, but that contact has not led to a campaign.

   If this number is low, you need to put more effort into increasing the size of your prospect list. (The chapter "The 10,000 Prospect Strategy" will give you ideas on how to increase your prospect-list size.)

3. Join Page Traffic

Tracking visits to you join page on your website allows you to test the effectiveness of your lead-generation tactics.

You can experiment with different website URLs in a leaflet or advertisement to measure the effectiveness of each of your lead-generation tactics.

4. Number of Inside Committees Set Up

5. Leads from Members

6. Testimonials Collected from Members

7. Members Enrolled in Organizing Courses

    Sending members to organizing courses is a great way to build a culture of organizing in your local.

Action Exercise: Measuring Your Outreach Efforts

1. Look at your past organizing efforts and work backwards.

    To meet your goal for number of workplaces organized, how many organizing leads would you need to generate this year?

2. Create a spreadsheet to track active campaigns, your prospect list, join page traffic, number of inside committees, leads from members and members through organizing classes

3. Review this spreadsheet regularly to find your area of opportunity. Is it winning votes? Is it setting up inside committees? Is it getting to a vote?

Chapter 4: Creating an Online Lead Generation Machine

When workers search "join a union" or "unions in Nevada," is your union showing up?

The easiest way to get more organizing leads faster and jumpstart your outreach efforts is to improve your online presence.

More workers view your union's organizing webpage than read your leaflets or speak to one of your organizers.

This means union organizers need to fundamentally change how they use the Internet to connect with workers.

How does your organizing webpage compare with your organizing leaflets in production quality, persuasiveness and the time you spend on it?

How good is your union at getting organizing leads through your website?

Best Practices for Union Websites

On average, most union websites convert one per cent of all visitors into organizing leads.

This means if your join page gets 500 visits then on average you will get 5 organizing leads.

If you could boost that number to three per cent, by using best practices other unions are currently using to get organizing leads online - you would triple the number of organizing leads you get in a year.

When workers visit your website you have only a split second to get their attention. It doesn't matter how persuasive your website copy is if potential members aren't reading past the first paragraph.

Best Practice Checklist

☐ Does your webpage have a hero shot?

Your hero shot is a picture of your ideal prospective member appearing as they would on the job.

It shows prospective members at a glance that they're at the right place and that this is a union for workers like them.

A retail worker might not be sure if the "United Food and

Commercial Workers" is a union for cashiers by the name alone. However, if they see a photo of another retail worker - they will stay on the page to learn more.

- If you're organizing electricians then have a photo of an electrician at work.

- If organizing nurses, have a photo of a nurse.

- If you're organizing security guards have a photo of a security guard in uniform.

Having a hero shot is particularly important if the classification of workers you are organizing isn't in your union's name.

☐ Do you have a clear and direct headline at the top of the page?

Examples of clear and direct headlines

- If you want fairness and respect at work, join our union

- Are you a retail worker who is sick of putting up with a bad manager?

- Learn more about joining a union in Nevada

Examples of poor headlines are:

- PICPA, more than 100 years of servicing Nevada

- Organizing

- Learn more

The role of your headline isn't just to describe your page - it's to get people to read the first sentence of your website copy.

☐ Does your website demonstrate credibility?

Workers are making a big decision to call you about forming a union at their workplace.

They might feel scared or unsure as to what will happen next.

If your website is out of date, looks like it was made by "a guy who knows a guy" or says "Copyright 2008", prospective members won't see you as credible.

☐ Does your join page have testimonials?

The "join page" should have testimonials with pictures or videos to demonstrate that the union is comprised of regular people.

The best testimonials are videos of members that look like your "joiner persona" (see Chapter 2).

The testimonials should not just promote being a part of your union - they should promote picking up the phone and calling an organizer.

For example, "When we first talked about joining a union we were a little scared, but we knew what was going on at work wasn't right. We didn't even know what our rights were; we thought you could be fired for joining a union. Then we met with Frank, an organizer with the union, and he led us through the process of forming a union at the plant. The difference now is like night and day - I'd never go back."

☐ Does your website have case studies?

You could prepare case studies on

- Organizing victories
- Progress in your major contracts
- Before-and-after stories of organized units

Some people have emotional triggers - others are more analytical. While testimonials help people with emotional triggers, case studies help convince the more analytical personalities.

☐ Do you have a "join" page rather than an "organizing" page?

Do you have an "organize" or "organizing" page on your site?

The language that we use matters.

Union staff use words like "organizing a union," "organizing departments" and "organizing drives."

Workers use words like "starting a union," "forming a union" and "joining a union."

It is possible that non-union workers may not even know that "organize" means join a union.

A recent search on Google showed that 42,000 people had typed, "join a union" into Google last month, whereas only 1,900 searched for "organize a union".

If you have a tab in your union's navigation that reads, "Organizing," change it to "Join our Union." That's what non-union workers are looking for anyways.

☐ Do you have a clear call to action?

When a worker finishes reading your join page, is there a clear call to action telling them what to do next?

Do you have a "contact us" button?

This is the online equivalent of asking for a commitment.

Good examples of calls to action are

- "contact us in confidence"

- "find out more about joining our union."

☐ Do you have a persuasive message above your call to action?

A final persuasive message just above the call to action will increase the response rates on your join page.

Look at the following two real-life examples that appeared above a "contact us" button.

Good: "Find out more about how joining the IBEW will help further your career in the electrical industry."

Bad: "Someone from our membership development team will either contact you or forward your information to the right person."

☐ Can workers contact you online?

From unions that track their website statistics – we know that the majority of visits to "join" pages occur during the weekend, or after 5 p.m. on weekdays.

This means that the time workers are most interested in joining a union is the same time you aren't at your office.

I was working with a union in California to create an online system to generate organizing leads when we came across a surprising discovery.

More than 40 people had called the toll-free number during the first weekend after the project launched.

The problem: <u>only four people left a message</u>

That suggests about 90 per cent of workers who wanted to join a union wouldn't leave a message on an unknown voicemail, especially when they aren't sure if their jobs were protected.

If people don't feel comfortable leaving messages after hours, you should provide them with an online option to contact you.

☐ Do you have Google Analytics on your Website?

Google Analytics is a free program that shows you how prospective members interact with your website.

While Google Analytics displays graphs showing the numbers of prospective members that visit your site, it can do much more.

You can use it to answer questions like:

- What does a first-time visitor look at on your join pages compared to a second-time visitor?
- How much time is a person spending to read the content of the website? (Do you have too much material or too little?)
- When do people leave your website? The first page? The FAQ page? While filling out the form?
- What is the most popular content on your site?

- What are people typing into Google to find your join page?
- Did people who applied to join look at different webpages than people who didn't apply?

Let's say you wanted to test if spending money on radio ads promoting joining your union was a good use of resources.

If you run your ads in a particular city, Google Analytics can display changes in traffic to your website in that city compared with previous months in the same city.

You could also test a unique website URL for your radio ads to see how many visitors and leads the advertising generated.

Using Google Analytics you could even test things like:

- Do colour leaflets perform better than black and white?
- How much text is the right amount for an organizing leaflet?

Let's say you have a budget of $10,000 for a mail drop campaign about joining a union.

Before spending $10,000, you might want to send $200 worth of black-and-white mail pieces with short text, $200 worth of colour pieces with short text and $200 worth of black-and-white pieces with longer text.

If each leaflet had a different website address, you could measure the traffic from each URL and learn:

- What is the best use of money – colour or black and white?
- Did the long or short text produce a better response rate?
- Did you get the results you wanted after spending $600? If not, the $10,000 campaign would have been a waste of resources.

☐ Are you testing versions of your website to see what is working and what isn't?

Did you know that some unions are using programs that allows your website to "learn" from visitors and make improvements to help convert your website traffic into organizing leads?

These programs create two versions of your website with a slight change on each. Half your visitors see version "A" and half version "B." At the end of the test, the system determines which version performed better.

Small changes - sometimes a single word on a page - can make dramatic changes in the number of people who contact your union.

One union I assisted doubled the number of people who contacted them online by slightly changing a single sentence.

They changed, "Joining a union is your right and you can't be fired," to, "Joining a union is confidential - you cannot be fired or disciplined."

Changing those words cost the union nothing and generated twice as many organizing leads for the local.

You should consider such change as:

- A new photo for your "hero shot"
- Different headlines on a page
- New text on buttons

The real value of program like Google Website Optimizer or Visual Website Optimizer is that you can run thousands of these experiments at once so that your website is constantly improving.

☐ Do you have a clear structure for your join page?

When it comes to website copy, less is more.

Content should flow smoothly with one section logically leading to another.

☐ Do the questions on your "join page" ask for anything more than basic information?

Some unions have online sign-up forms that require information like employer address or the worker's home address.

Your website content should not scare off prospective members.

The time and place to ask questions like "how many people work there" and "what products does your company make" is when you sit down with the prospective member face to face.

Unions that have reduced the number of pieces of information they ask for report the number of signings increase by about 75 per cent.

Workers are already scared enough about contacting a union – don't increase their anxiety.

The only purpose of your sign-up form should be to get to the meeting. You can ask your questions then.

☐ **Do you emphasize that contacting a union is confidential?**

Emphasizing confidentiality will increase the number of prospective members who will contact you.

The Most Important Number

You should concentrate on one number when it comes to getting organizing leads from your website.

It's not the number of visits to the website.

It's not the average length of each visit.

It's the conversion rate - the percentage of website visitors who contact you about joining a union.

The Three-Per-Cent Challenge

Most unions convert around one per cent of all visitors into organizing leads.

Do you think you can raise the number from one per cent to three? It wouldn't be that difficult and it would mean tripling the number of leads you generate from your website.

Split Testing is the Key to Increasing Your Conversion Rate

Split testing is showing different webpages that are different in only one aspect.

Half of visitors see headline A and half of visitors see headline B. You look at which headline brought you the highest number of organizing leads and pick that headline as the winner so that future visitors see the best headline.

The real power of split testing is that you can run many of these tests simultaneously.

You could test different headlines, different photos, different colours, different fonts or different messages.

To split test your website you can use programs like Google's Website Optimizer or Visual Website Optimizer.

If you don't get the technology, that's ok, just hire someone who does.

Remember that your website is your most read piece of organizing campaign literature so it is worth spending time on it.

Creating Persuasive Website Copy

The good news is you don't have to be a great writer to create an online lead generating machine.

The best way to come up with content is to put yourself in a prospective member's shoes and think of the questions they might ask if you were to sit down with them for coffee.

Creating a Feedback System

Adding a "feedback" or "questions" button on your website can make your webpage more effective.

It gives prospective members an opportunity to tell you exactly why they didn't contact you.

If you start to see a trend in questions workers ask, address it on your website and see if the number of leads you get increases.

Two popular and free services for adding feedback on your website are "KISS Insights" and "4Q."

Secondary Calls to Action

A secondary call to action is a question seen as a "lower risk" than requesting a meeting with an organizer.

It might be

- Requesting a guide to joining a union in your state or province in exchange for an email address
- A PDF download of 10 things you need to know about joining a union in exchange for an email address
- An "ask-a-question" form at the bottom of your page

Turning Secondary Call to Action Visitors into Leads

Once you have the email address for the prospective member, slowly send them value over time to make the prospective member feel more comfortable with joining your union.

You could send them:

- Articles from local papers about the advantages of being a union member
- A document that outlines their rights to join a union in your area
- Testimonials or case studies that answer questions they have on their mind

The key is that whatever you send them must be <u>relevant</u> and <u>valuable.</u>

After you send a couple of valuable articles, you could follow up with an email such as:

Subject: What does your week look like?

Hi (NAME),

"I saw that you downloaded the guide the other day about joining a union in Nova Scotia.

I'm busy Tuesday and Thursday, but are you free to meet this Wednesday at 1pm?"

Learning from Others

Go to Google and search "join a union" "start a union" or "form a union."

Look at websites that you find and rate them against the framework discussed in this chapter.

- Do they use any of the best practices?
- What are they doing right that you should copy?
- What are they doing wrong that you should avoid?

Creating Persuasive Website Content

Your best source of website content is your own organizers.

The way they speak in a one-on-one conversation is exactly the conversational tone and information that needs to be conveyed to your prospective members through your website.

Try recording a role-play session with your union organizers.

Go around the room and create a list of common objections to joining a union or common obstacles that hold workers back from contacting a union.

Put each of these items in a hat and draw them out one by one, answering each question.

(The answers to these questions would make a great FAQ section for your join site.)

Separate Websites for Each Sector

You should create separate websites for each audience you are trying to reach.

Once you have created your outreach message, make sure you are directing the right message to the right audience.

Your union may represent a diverse membership, but it's important to show messages and photos that are directed specifically at the group you are trying to organize rather than "workers" in general.

Health-care workers respond very well to messages about being treated as health-care professionals, but security guards would not.

Don't Ignore Prospective Members Over the Weekend

Create a system to ensure that if someone contacts you Friday night, they don't have to wait until Monday afternoon to hear back from you.

One way to accomplish this is by using an auto-responder.

If you've ever received an "out of office reply" to an email, then you've seen an auto-responder.

When someone fills in an online form to join your union, you need to send them pieces of information as soon as possible so they know their request has been received.

It helps reduce some of the anxiety of people who contact you.

What Should You Say in an Auto-Responder?

The best thing to send is valuable information.

- Send a list of the top 10 questions about joining a union.
- Send a video outlining their right to join a union in your province or state.

Whatever you send them you must give prospective members confidence so that they don't duck your call on Monday out of fear.

The easiest way to set up an auto-responder is to set up a separate email account at your office for organizing leads.

Rather than setting the out-of-office reply to, "I'm out of the office but you can reach me at . . . ," set it to, "Hi, thanks for your interest in joining our union. We've put together a list of the 10 most common questions people have about forming a union at work that you can download here. Our office reopens Monday and someone will give you a call then."

Organizing Website Mistakes

One common mistake is the one-page join page with text about how great the union is, how long they've been in existence and the name of the union's organizer?

These pages tend to lack a strong call to action, or any persuasive text that makes prospective members want to take action.

Could you imagine if an advertising agency tried to sell shoes using this type of page?

Here is what I think it would look like if based on a union's organizing page I came across last night.

Headline: Sales Department

Body: Nike Shoes has been serving Oregon since 1964. Our professional staff can help you with anything you need.

Our salesperson Philip Knight has worked for the company for 10 years and his email is pknight@nike.com.

If you have any questions about buying shoes, please call our salesperson Phillip Knight at 555-XXX-XXXX.

Another common join page mistake is the "brochure site"

This is a page with several points about the union - maybe some nice pictures of the office building - but nothing that creates desire, overcomes barriers or persuades someone to call your union.

If a brochure site was a union organizer she would knock on a prospective member's door, tell the worker just a bit about the union, and then politely turn around and leave without asking for commitment or someone to sign a card.

The only purpose of your organizing webpage should be to persuade people to fill in an online form to request a meeting or call you.

Actions Exercises

1. Install Google Analytics and Google Website Optimizer. They're both free.

2. Get an idea of how effective you are right now at generating leads. Use Google Analytics to determine your conversion rate (the percentage of visitors who actually contact you.)

3. Change your current pages using the best practices outlined in this document and see if you can at least triple your conversion rate.

4. Split test your website continuously to improve how many leads you can generate.

To watch an online video with more ideas on creating organizing websites go to http://www.PromotingYourUnion.com

Chapter 5: Getting Organizing Leads at Strategic Targets Through Agitation/Education Campaigns

The way to approach strategic targets is different from a hot shop because you cannot afford to leave burnt turf.

The worst way to approach strategic targets is cold leafleting.

- The employer knows about your campaign before you can set up an inside committee.
- The conversation in the workplace about the union starts to happen as soon as you start the cold leafleting, but you can't join this conversation because you don't have an employee list.

Trying to cold leaflet without an inside committee or a firm list is setting yourself up for failure before you start.

Cold leafleting is a bit like proposing marriage to strangers in a bar.

The law of probability suggests that if you ask enough people someone eventually might say yes, but proposing marriage to random people in a bar isn't a great strategy even if it works occasionally.

How many times have you sat down for a first inside committee meeting and heard a story about how another union once stood outside their workplace, but left two weeks later when they hadn't signed any cards?

These situations make people cynical and jaded about union organizing, and you can't afford to alienate workers at your strategic targets.

While communicating with workers at strategic targets on a regular basis is a great idea, standing outside of a worksite with a leaflet saying, "join our union" isn't the only way to do it.

Why Not Advertise?

Using traditional advertising for union organizing is expensive and untargeted.

Advertising to workers at strategic targets creates another problem - it plays into the employer's hand and gives the employer room to say:

"Look at how much money the union is spending to get you to join. They wouldn't do it if there weren't a lot of money in it for them. A union is a business and they are advertising today so they can get your dues money tomorrow."

Creating a "Pull campaign" Instead of a "Push campaign"

One of the best ways to avoid being labeled as a third party is to have workers come to you rather than you going to them.

Does this mean you should just sit in your office until workers knock on your door and tell you they're ready to be organized?

No, it just means that "sign a card and join our union today" isn't the only message an organizer can communicate to workers.

The alternative is an agitation/education campaign, which works like a magnet to bring workers to you.

While unions are eager to pursue leads at strategic targets, starting an organizing drive just because one person at one worksite approaches you is a poor plan.

The timing may not be right, the contact may not be the right person to help lead a campaign, or there may not be a burning reason in the unit that makes workers wiling to organize.

Agitate -> Educate -> Organize

With strategic targets, we sometimes make the mistake of trying to organize a unit prior to doing any agitation or educational work.

Unfortunately some unions take the attitude that if cards aren't being signed after standing outside a plant gate for a couple weeks, the fault is with the workers and the union will just try again a year later.

A better approach with long-term strategic targets is to first run an agitation campaign, and wait until the time is right for an organizing campaign.

How to Run an Agitation Campaign

During an agitation campaign your goal is to create a conversation on a union issue in the workplace that spreads quickly.

Some examples:

- "Do you think it is fair that you get paid $3 less than the people who work down the street?"
- "Why are managers at a retreat in Mexico while wages at the plant are frozen?"
- "Do you think the millennium project should be scrapped?"

The more specific your message, the more likely it will go viral.

Putting out a leaflet about respect in general won't likely spread, but detailing specific situations that show a lack of respect might.

Look for Broadly Felt Issues - Not Petty Complaints

The issues you pick for an agitation campaign must be moral, widely felt by the workers and speak to a union issue. Avoid siding with "complainers."

If you pick an issue that isn't widely felt then your agitation campaign comes across as the union being a bunch of whiners.

Where Can You Find These Issues?

If you don't already have contacts at the worksite, a great source of information for agitation campaigns are employer-review websites.

These are websites where employees and former employees post reviews about what it was like to work for a particular company. If you dig deeply on these sites you can start to piece together a pattern and find issues that are widely felt.

Let's say you discover your strategic target has rolled out a new program called the Millennium Project that speeds up the workflow and has decreased morale.

You could put together an agitation leaflet like the following to distribute outside of the workplace.

"Do you think the millennium project should be scrapped?

Yes? No?

Visit millenniumproject.com to vote and give your opinion."

Why This Works

Unlike a cold leaflet, where you present a solution that not everyone is yet seeking, this leaflet taps into something people care about deeply.

It gives the "no" and "yes" side equal motivation to go read your material. People won't feel disloyal about going online to vote because the leaflet treats both sides as valid. (Yet because of the way the question is phrased, it is likely the "yes" side will drown out the "no" side)

You can collect contact information. You could set up your system so people have to provide their email to make a comment, or maybe you could have a voting button with one vote per email address.

You have the ability to come back a couple weeks later with a leaflet containing the results of the vote.

What to Avoid During the Agitation Campaign

After starting to build a list and creating a buzz in the workplace, many unions who have tried the agitation campaign strategy have made the mistake of moving to an organizing drive prematurely.

The idea is to first agitate then educate and then organize.

If you ask people to join your union during the agitation stage, you will come off as self-serving.

Management will respond by saying, "The union is just here because they want your dues."

However, if you wait to organize until the conditions are right, management will either be forced into a position to defend an unpopular program or be seen to be backing down to the union's demands.

Either way you win.

Union busters are skilled at fighting off traditional organizing drives. They've seen the same tactics repeatedly. What they wont be expecting - and don't have the tools to fight off - is an agitation campaign.

Testing the Waters

If you have a few strategic organizing targets and aren't sure if the time is right for an organizing drive - running an agitation campaign is a good way to determine whether a workplace is ready for an organizing campaign.

Pay attention to the response to your agitation campaign.

If you used a tactic like asking workers to vote on a particular policy of an employer, the result of the vote is a good proxy for how they might accept an organizing drive at their workplace.

The Best Possible Outcome

The other goal of an agitation campaign is to provoke management to respond and put them on the defensive.

Experienced organizers know that the side always on the defensive usually loses the campaign.

Force Management to Respond Early

Getting management to respond is often the best way to get your message to go viral.

For example, if you distribute leaflets about how a particular new policy shows a lack of respect, and management responds with a letter saying, "The union is wrong; we do respect you," you win.

Chapter 6: The 10,000 Prospect Strategy

While creating an online campaign for a union – I realized that the names of the signers on our petition list represented a list of workers without a union in the sector we were organizing.

If you had a contact database of non-union workers in your sector it would make a difference in the number of people you could organize this year.

In this chapter, I'll show you how to build a list of 10,000 qualified prospects in your target industry and how to do it quickly and cheaply.

Touchpoints in Union Organizing Lead Generation

It takes several touchpoints (points of contact) to give workers the confidence to approach you about joining a union.

Employers have created a workplace climate and legislative environment where joining a union is a risk rather than a right.

Prospective members need reassurance, education and trust that takes time to build.

This is one of the main problems with cold leafleting.

With cold leafleting, you get one touchpoint and as soon as you are outside the plant gate, union busters will be on a jet flying to the plant.

The problem is it often takes four to six exposures with your message to give workers the confidence to contact your organizers.

Why Traditional Advertising to Generate Leads is Usually a Waste of Money

How can you get five or six exposures with a prospective member?

You could try print advertising, TV or radio ads, but the cost to get four to six touchpoints with a qualified prospective member would be unreasonable because most of your advertising budget would be spent advertising to people who are not in your sector.

If you ran TV ads targeting electricians in California, you would succeed in reaching non-union electricians, but most of your money would be wasted on advertising to people who are not electricians.

There isn't a way to know if your efforts are working with traditional advertising, which means you won't know if your ad is creating any impact until the money is already spent.

Direct-Response Marketing with Email

In contrast to traditional advertising platforms, email is an easy and inexpensive way to keep in touch with thousands of workers in the non-union sector.

More important, by using email to build a relationship with your list, you know the money you spend is all going to your target audience.

The challenge is building a large targeted list.

The Degree of Your Success

The number of leads you generate will be directly proportional to the size of your contact list and how targeted it is.

A list of 500 workers is unlikely to generate many leads.

A large list of workers that is untargeted isn't special either. That's just the phone book.

However, if you can build a list of 10,000 prospective members that are in your sector and get even one per cent of those people to give you a call, it could change your local.

How to Build a Contact Database

There are six sources from which your union can easily build a large contact database of non-union workers:

1. Former Members of Your Union

   Just because someone leaves their job doesn't mean they leave the sector.

   A care-aide at a unionized nursing home that leaves her job likely will end up at a non-union care facility. Your union needs a systematic method to keep in touch with former members.

   Add former members to your contact database and continue to build a relationship with them.

2. Card Signers from Unsuccessful Organizing Drives

   Adding card signers to your list of non-union contacts is a great way to keep in touch.

   If they stay at their job - you will have a head start if you restart an organizing campaign at that worksite.

   If they leave their job – you will have a contact at a non-union employer that has expressed interest in joining a union and is familiar with the organizing process.

3. Exchanging Contact Information for Valuable Information

   A quick way to build a targeted list of non-union workers in your sector is to create a list of the best paying unionized employers in the industry.

   Place the list on your website and offer it for download in exchange for an email address.

If you wanted to organize security guards, you could create a list of the best unionized security firms in the industry and advertise that you have the list available for download on job search sites.

You will quickly build up a list of security guards in your area.

If they find work at a place you already have a certification – great. The new member will appreciate that you helped them out.

If they find a job in the non-union sector - they will remember that there are better paying jobs in union firms and that there is a union for security guards.

4. Campaigning Among Non-Union Workers

The fastest way to build a targeted list is to create an issue-based campaign that appeals to your target organizing audience.

By tying your list-building effort to a demand or campaign, you can engage with prospective members about an issue that interests them.

It also demonstrates that the union doesn't just fight for its members, but for the working conditions of everyone in the sector rather than workers as a whole.

The campaign must be closely linked to your audience so you are signing up workers in your sector.

- If you are organizing retail workers, you could petition for a longer minimum call-out or a living wage.

- If you are organizing nursing homes, you could campaign for respect for care aides.
- If you are organizing child-care providers, you could demand a quality public child-care system.

How much your demand or resonates with your audience will determine your success in getting more workers to sign up.

The best campaigns or demands motivate your target audience to take action and spread the campaign among their non-union friends in the sector.

Creating a Viral List-Building System for Your List Building Campaigns

Think of your website as a list-building machine. Its sole purpose is to build a list and collect information for follow up.

Later, you can educate prospective members about your campaign and show them ways to get involved and the advantages of becoming a member of your union.

Some unions make the mistake of creating websites that are "pretty" or "flashy" but do not accomplish the main task of collecting information for follow up and organizing.

Great List-Building Pages

In testing and optimizing campaign websites the most effective sites tend to have the following.

1. A photo or video of a person from the sector you are targeting

    If the campaign is for care aides, then prominently display a picture of a care aide.

2. A large and clear headline

    The central demand of your campaign should appear prominently on the top of your page.

3. A clear call to action and explain the demands of the campaign or petition in a few lines

4. A large "sign" or "I support respect for care aides" button rather than a small "submit" button

5. A privacy statement that assures people their information will be protected and not shared

Constantly Improve the Sign-Up Page

A surprising thing about list-building pages that I've set up for unions with the 10,000 prospect strategy is that small changes make big differences to the number of people who will sign up and share the list building campaign with their friends.

One union I assisted had a sign-up page that converted only six per cent of its traffic into petition signers, but was able to increase the conversion rate to 20 per cent by making small tweaks.

We noticed a high number of visitors left the website within two seconds of arriving. I suggested that we try tweaking elements that people look at in the first two seconds – the headline and main graphic.

The union took 10 new pictures to test on the site.

Looking at the 10 pictures, it would be impossible to tell which one would be most effective in encouraging people to sign up to the campaign, but when we tested each picture we found that the winning picture outperformed the original 2 to 1.

How to Run Tests on Your Campaign Site

Getting 10 times the traffic to your campaign website is hard.

Tweaking a page so that it is 10 times more effective at capturing an email address is easy.

Two programs let you run these types of tests on your website.

One is Google Website Optimizer. Like many products from Google, it is free, but it does require that you know a bit of HTML code.

Alternatively, you can use another program called Visual Website Optimizer. This program is not free, but you don't have to know any HTML code in order to edit or make changes to your website.

These programs allow you to test different versions of your website to see which works better at signing up prospects.

For example, you could test five different pictures on your campaign site, five different "submit" buttons, five versions of website copy, or five versions of a headline.

Getting the List to Grow Itself

Many unions set up great capture pages for their campaigns, but fall short in persuading people who have signed up to help spread the campaign.

It isn't an exaggeration to suggest that by not providing tools to people who have signed onto your campaign you are missing up to 80 per cent of possible contacts.

Leveraging Sign-ups with the Thank-You Page

Let's say - for easy math – that you could get a quarter of the people who signed your petition or supported your campaign to sign up two more people by sending their friends a personal message by email or social media.

That means that if you initially signed up 100 people, and 25 of those people got two more to sign up, you'd have 150 sign-ups in total.

However, it doesn't stop there.

Sharing works in the same way as compound interest – the increases build on themselves.

The additional 50 contacts will sign up 25 additional people. Those 25 people bring in 13 more and those 13 bring in seven more. It keeps going until eventually in total you've signed up 197 people.

Because you gave an option to share and 25% of people shared with two people, you turned 100 prospects into almost 200.

Getting 25% of people to share is easy, and the good news is that small changes can have significant impacts on the compounding.

Let's say you put a little bit of time into it and optimized the system so you got 40 per cent of people to share with two friends.

Let's look at that math.

If 100 people sign up to your list and 40% share with two people, you will get an additional 80 contacts. Again, like compound interest, those 80 names will give you an additional 64 names. Those 64 people will give you about 50 names, those 50 will give you 40, the 40 will give you 32, etc. It will keep growing until eventually you'll have 460 prospects in total.

Focus on Optimizing the Sharing System

What if you focused on improving your sharing page through split testing and made another modest change so that 45% of people who sign up share with two others?

Here's how the math would work:

If you sign up 100 people initially and 45% of those people share with two others, you would have an additional 90 sign-ups.

Those 90 sign up 81 and the 81 sign up 72, etc. It will keep building until, in the end, the total will be 892 prospects.

By increasing the share rate by a small amount, you've doubled the number of names collected.

The Thank-You Page

The key to getting signers to invite their friends is the thank-you page.

Some unions don't take advantage of the page that appears immediately after a prospect fills in a form.

Their thank-you page may say: "Thanks for signing," or "Your signature has been confirmed," or "Form submission confirmed."

What a wasted opportunity.

Your thank-you page should be a persuasive communications piece designed to encourage people to share the campaign with their friends.

Your thank you page should say something like, "Thanks for supporting our campaign. Five thousand other child-care providers in the state have already supported the campaign by spreading this campaign to their friends. Can you help us by sharing this campaign with five friends?"

Specific One-Click Asks

The easier and more specific your request, the more likely someone will take the action you are asking him or her to take.

On your thank-you page, don't just put up a headline that says, "Please spread this to your friends" - instead put a big giant button right on the page that with one click posts the campaign to their Facebook page or emails the petition to five friends.

The thank-you page is the most important page in creating a viral list-building machine and, just as you did with your organizing website, you should optimize your thank-you page with Google Website Optimizer or Visual Website Optimizer.

- You could try five different calls to action.
- You could try five different versions of a Facebook button.
- You could try five different pictures.
- You could try five different types of social proof.

It doesn't take an elaborate or expensive system to build a viral list-building machine that you can use to build a targeted prospect list.

It takes a petition page optimized to get visitors to sign and a thank-you page optimized to encourage signers to ask their friends to sign.

How One Person Can Generate a List of 10,000 Prospects

If you can create a system optimized for sharing and email the link to your membership, you should not have any problem getting 10,000 prospects.

If you could get 2,000 of your own members to join in and spread the word to their friends, that's more than enough to get the ball rolling.

What Should You Send Out to the Prospect List?

Here are the keys to get organizing leads from your prospect list:

1. Don't talk about yourself

    Don't directly ask people to join your union - at least not at first.

    Right now they don't know about you and don't care about you.

    Coming on too strong is a sure way to land your emails in their spam box.

    It takes at least five touchpoints with somebody to get them comfortable about joining your union.

    The first messages you send to a prospective member should

be relevant to the demands of the campaign. By positioning your union as caring about the same things the prospective member does, you will build trust in your organization.

The best way to do this is set up a series of automated messages, also known as a drip-marketing campaign.

In a drip marketing campaign - potential members are automatically sent a message on the first day they sign up, then get a message three days later, then another one five days later.

With 10,000 prospects on your list, it can be time-consuming to send out these emails, but programs like MailChimp, Aweber and Constant Contact can automate this process for you.

2. Send valuable pieces of information

After you have sent out a few emails about the campaign, you can transition into sending emails that are valuable to recipients but inexpensive to you.

It could be a list of the best-paying unionized employers in your industry or a research piece written by someone in your union.

It could also be industry news or stories from other people like your prospective member.

The test of whether something is valuable is, "Will they be happy that you sent it to them?" The key is to build a relationship slowly over time through value-based messages.

3. Introduce your union

   After you've sent out a few valuable pieces of information, you can start positioning your union.

   The best way to start talking about your union without looking like a salesperson is through third-party articles.

   You could send out occasional news reports covering positive stories about your union or stories from members or testimonials along with valuable pieces of information.

   You could send out op-ed pieces written by your union president on an issue of interest to the prospective member.

4. Turn prospects into leads

   After you've provided value to prospective members and started to introduce your union, you can start the process of turning prospects into leads.

   Keep in mind that direct pitches turn people off and it will lead to people blocking your messages or unsubscribing from your list.

   While you want to get organizing leads from prospective members today, you don't want to turn people off by being pushy.

   Just because someone isn't ready to join your union today, there may be a situation six months down the road when they have a problem at work. If you've been sending them the occasional valuable message, you will be on the top of their mind.

   The best way to get people to join your union without

directly asking them to join is to send emails that link to interesting articles on your union's website related to the campaign. At the bottom of the article, place a call to action about joining your union.

To watch an online video on the 10,000 Prospect Strategy go to http://www.PromotingYourUnion.com

Chapter 7: Using Facebook to Get Organizing Leads

Here is how to start an organizing drive using Facebook:

- Use Facebook to create an employee list.
- Find issues that resonate in the workplace.
- Set up a Facebook page for employees.
- Get more people to join your Facebook page.
- Take out Facebook advertising.
- Use Facebook for list-building campaigns.

Step One: Using Facebook to Create Employee Lists

Facebook is a great tool to put together employee lists, map out a workplace or find demographics on workers at your strategic targets.

Collecting employee names is easy because of the amount of personal information people put on Facebook.

For example, if you search for "Wal-Mart 5834" or "Wal-Mart Terrace," you will find a partial employee list that could be the basis for the beginning of a campaign.

Using Facebook Search

1. Visit http://www.facebook.com/search/
2. Click "groups"
3. Type the name of the employer

You probably won't find an entire employee list, maybe just 10 per cent of employees of a given company. However, it's a start.

A Caution

Once you have a list of names, you might be tempted to send this group a message - don't.

Contacting someone you do not know through Facebook has a stigma.

A better approach is to take the list of names and run it against an online database like whitepages.com to find contact information.

Getting Phone Numbers and Addresses

If your union has a database of members and past members, you could check the names against it to see if there are any former members.

Take your list to White Pages Professional

(http://pro.whitepages.com). This service allows you to take your first name/last name list, upload it to WhitePages Pro by location and find all phone numbers and addresses associated with the names. While there is a small cost for using this program, it only charges you for the names, phone numbers and addresses it finds and it's far less expensive than your time to enter all of those names manually into a free service like 411.com.

Could you imagine what you could do if you searched every Wal-Mart store in North America and then made a mailing list of Wal-Mart employees?

Step Two: Find issues that resonate in the workplace

In step one, you built employee lists from information you gathered on Facebook.

You got the phone numbers and addresses of these workers from the information you researched on WhitePages Pro.

Facebook allows you to find out what is really going on at a workplace.

You can find issues that really matter to workers at your target employer so you don't have to guess what might be happening when you reach out to the first people on your contact list.

Read the different employee Facebook groups regularly to find out what is happening day to day at the workplace.

Often the little things make workers look for a union solution.

It might be scheduling, a new policy or a new manager.

Facebook is an excellent source of this information.

A Caution (Part 2)

You might be tempted to jump into these employee groups and post information about how great your union is - don't!

Don't say, "Hey, I'm Joe from the union and any worker who would like to join can contact me at . . . "

It won't work and will likely scare people off.

Information in Status Updates

You can also find out what people have posted onto pages or groups and what people are posting on their status updates through Facebook search.

1. Go to http://www.Facebook.com/search/
2. Click "Posts by Everyone"

3. Type your search term

Step 3: Setting up Facebook Pages

If you can't find any groups set up by employees at a worksite then create a Facebook page for employees to gather.

Creating chain-based or employer-based Facebook pages is one of the most powerful tools a union organizer can use on Facebook to generate new leads.

How to Start a Facebook Page

1. Choose a name for your page (i.e.: "I work at Comcast")
2. Visit http://www.Facebook.com/Pages/ and register the group

Why a Facebook Page Rather than a group?

With a Facebook page, you can develop a relationship with people who join by publishing status updates that go directly to users of the page.

Facebook pages also allow you to see the demographic information about the people who join your page. This information can be invaluable to other communications efforts of your campaign.

If you are organizing Comcast, you could start a page called, "I work at Comcast."

If you're organizing traffic controller workers in New York, set up a page called, "NYC Flaggers."

Things to do With a Facebook Page You Set Up

1. Build employee lists.
2. Target your advertising to members and friends on your Facebook page.
3. Test various messages.

Go to a job review site like JobVent.com or RateMyEmployer.ca and find out what people are saying about their workplace or look for common trends.

Post common issues onto your Facebook page as status updates to see which issues seem to resonate with the group.

You can also find things to post based on the research you did in step two.

For example, you discover Staples has a problem with giving performance reviews on time. You could ask members of your "I work at Staples" page, "Who here got their last performance review on time?"

A Caution (Part 3)

You might be temped to post status updates like, "You can join

IBEW by visiting http://www.ibew.org/contact ."

If you bombard people with hard asks before you demonstrate value or build a relationship, people will be turned off.

No One is Interested in You... At Least Not Yet

The opportunity of setting up Facebook pages isn't to bombard people with requests to join your union. It's to demonstrate value so that people will want to join your union.

You will find the softer the message, the better.

Your goal is to encourage interaction. Building a relationship is a slow process that can't be rushed.

It's not the number of fans you have in your Facebook page; it's the level of interaction that matters.

Converting Facebook Fans into Organizing Leads

Ask questions and identify supporters and leaders. People love to give their opinions.

Your job is to ask questions that turn workers towards thinking of a union solution the next time they have a problem at work.

You can then identify potential supporters based on the answers to the questions that you ask.

You can build a survey right into the Facebook page. The question could read:

Should COMPANYNAME have a union?

Yes? / No?

Email:

City:

Comments:

This question is great because you will identify many people who say yes and you can follow up with them.

Just an important, you can identify people who say no and determine what they have in common based on what they entered in the comments section. You can use the information to find out what obstacles are holding back this worksite from joining a union.

Post articles to your union's Facebook page from your union's website.

Let's say you ask the group, "Should traffic-control workers be paid a living wage like other workers in the construction industry?" and you see positive feedback.

You could then write an article on your union's website about how traffic-control workers should be paid a living wage.

Place a link to the article on your Facebook page and make sure the article contains some information about how to join your union at the bottom.

Step 4: Getting more people to join your Facebook page

The best way to grow your Facebook page is to encourage interaction. When workers interact with your Facebook page, it shows up on their Facebook profile, where their co-workers can see it.

Here are some keys to building interaction:

1. Set the "Wall" settings on Facebook to "display posts by page and fans." Allowing fans to publish directly to your wall and have their posts seen encourages people to respond and interact with each other. (You can change this setting at Edit Pages -> Wall settings -> Default view for Wall "All Posts").

2. Respond to every comment and post that fans make on your page.

3. Post a status update every two days.

4. Direct people to articles or conversation pieces that are valuable to them or resonate with people who joined your page.

    You could ask people to post a funny story about what happened to them while at work or poll people on certain topics.

5. Write a status update ask people to press "like" if they agree. If they disagree, ask them to comment why.

Prime the Pump

Once you start your Facebook page, it will grow very slowly unless you already have many non-union workers who are friends with you on Facebook that you can invite.

Facebook advertising allows targeting by employer. Use Facebook ads to advertise your fan page.

You can take out ads asking such questions as, "Do you work at Comcast? Become a fan."

Once you have several hundred workers join by advertising, you can work on increasing the interaction through the viral nature of your Facebook page.

Step 5: Facebook Advertising

The advantage of Facebook advertising for union organizers is the ability to target your ads by employer.

You can also target members of pages you have set up.

You can refine your targeting even further by targeting keywords that appear on a users' profile.

For example, you could target users who say they "like" Barack Obama. Those users are more likely to contact a union about joining than someone who "likes" Republicans.

If you wanted to organize workers at Comcast in Georgia, you would set targeting the following way:

Workplace: Comcast

State: Georgia

Keywords: Obama

(You can set up Facebook ads at http://www.Facebook.com/ads/create/ .)

Contacting a union directly off Facebook requires a lot of trust. If you were advertising a summer camp on Facebook, you'd have a much higher rate of success if you asked people to visit your website and download a free video about your camp rather than directly making the ask to register online to a camp they haven't heard of.

Similarly, you will have better results generating organizing leads if you advertise something of value that you will give free to non-union workers who click your advertisement.

It could be a free guide about how to join a union in your state or province. It could also be a petition to sign or free guide that contains the highest-paying union jobs in your industry in your region.

Advertising to Test Messaging

You can also use Facebook ads to test your campaign messages. I was once helping a union put together a campaign for traffic-control workers and build up a list of employees working at non-union traffic-control companies.

We had two campaign names we thought would succeed, but weren't sure which campaign would resonate better with traffic-control workers.

One was a campaign for respect and fairness; the other a campaign for a living wage for traffic-control workers.

Polling a group to find out the answer was one option, but expensive.

We had a group of 1,000 flaggers in a Facebook page we had established, so we set up advertising aimed at them.

Half saw a message asking them to get involved with the union around a campaign for respect and fairness.

The other half was shown a message relating to earning a living wage.

What was interesting was that the message revolving around respect and fairness got three times the response rate.

The total cost of the experiment was $10, but the information learned was invaluable.

(I also used Facebook ads to test the name for this book. $5 worth of ads showed me that union activists were more interested in "Promoting Your Union – six strategies to get more organizing leads and union members" than "Organize! Tactics and strategies to grow your union")

Step Six: Using Facebook for List-building Campaigns

By using a Facebook Application called FBML (Facebook Markup Language), you can place an email capture form directly on your Facebook page.

Here are two suggestions:

- Set up a petition around a campaign relevant to your target group.

  In our example of the traffic-control workers, you could set up a tab called, "Fairness for Flaggers." The petition could contain spaces for name, email address and employer.

- Create a list of the highest-paying jobs in your industry that a worker can download by giving you their email address.

  You could list employers with your best collective agreements. Not only does this tactic collect information from non-union employees, it demonstrates that union jobs are good jobs and helps build a relationship with non-union workers.

Action Exercise:

1. Brainstorm a list of potential employers.

2. Search for employee groups set up by Facebook users.

3. Make a first name/last name list sorted by worksite.

4. Upload your spreadsheet to WhitePages Pro to get contact information.

5. Bookmark employee Facebook groups of organizing targets and check them regularly for information.

6. Visit Facebook.com/search and regularly search the company name to find additional information.

7. Check out www.JobVent.com and RateMyEmployer.com to find out what types of issues you might want to discuss on Facebook.

8. Pick a name for an employer-based Facebook group, such as, "I work at McDonald's" or "McDonald's Employees California."

9. Set up your Facebook page at http://www.Facebook.com/Pages/

10. Ask open-ended questions to the group about their jobs, and issues you know are hot buttons from step seven.

11. Based on the responses, keep a list of any employees that might be good inside-committee members to contact.

12. Write articles on your union website based on the hot-button issues you identified through listening to Facebook users.

13. Place links on the Facebook page directing workers back to your union's website about an issue you know they feel strongly about.

14. Get more people to join your page by encouraging interaction.

15. Set your "wall settings" to display all posts.

16. Comment and respond to everyone who posts on your page.

17. Make status updates every two days to your page with a valuable article or question to start a conversation.

18. Take out Facebook advertising to prime the pump and get initial visitors to join your page.

19. Set up a Facebook advertising account at Facebook.com/ads/

20. Brainstorm what you could offer free that non-union workers would find valuable, such as a list of the top-paying jobs in the industry.

21. Advertise this "bait" piece on Facebook and drive people back to your union's website where they can download the article in exchange for an email.

22. Send valuable information over time to potential organizing leads.

To watch an online video on how to use Facebook to get organizing leads visit http://www.PromotingYourUnion.com

Chapter 8: Building a Relationship with Workers Before They Enter the Workforce

The Problem

Employers have more power than ever to interfere with workers' right to join a union.

Because of the fear associated with joining a union, we need to look for opportunities to start talking about unions in the community rather than at the factory gate.

A Radical Idea

Why should organizers wait until after workers enter the workforce before they try to build a relationship with them?

What would happen if we connected with future electricians, nurses, care aides, meat cutters and mechanics while they are in school?

Here are a few reasons your organizing department should speak to your future members before they enter the workforce:

- No fear of retaliation: At school, people are away from the prying eyes of employers. They can hear the difference your union makes without worrying about being fired.
- Trust building: In a cold campaign, organizers have a short time to build trust. Approaching possible future members in school starts the gradual process of building trust in unions.
- Incubate future leads: Collect contact information from students and give them a call after they enter the workforce.

Connecting with Students

It's not enough to have a single interaction, such as speaking in class; you need to get permission to follow up with these future workers before and after they enter the workforce.

You can't turn these contacts into organizing leads without this permission.

Here are some ways a nurses' union could connect with students. (With creativity, you could use these same tactics for care aides, meat cutters, pharmacy techs and a variety of other professions.)

- Industry nights: Book a room on campus and hold an industry night to let students know about trends and changes in the industry. Have a sign-in form at the front to collect information.

- Classroom speaking: Health-care unions are a part of a career in health care. Instructors would be happy to have you give a quick presentation to classes. Be sure to hand out contact forms for more information.

- Associate memberships: Have an associate-membership program for students. Associate members would be able to attend meetings and participate vocally. They would not vote, but would get communications from your union.

- Offer valuable information in exchange for contact information: Write a guide showing the top paying unionized employers in the industry. Get people to give you their name and email address - in person or on your website - in order to receive a free copy of the guide.

- Assist student societies and clubs: Build a relationship with related clubs and associations of nursing students on campus. A little money could go a long way.

- Scholarship opportunities: Set up a scholarship for nurses entering the profession.

By building a relationship with students and getting organizing leads, you're engaging workers in your industry before they enter the workforce and getting their permission to contact them when they enter the workforce.

If you have several hundred contacts, the only practical way to follow up, give value and build a relationship is by email.

Some points to keep in mind as you develop those relationships:

- Go Slow: It's like dating. You don't propose marriage on the first date; it takes time to build trust. Send one message immediately so your email address is recognized. Send another email about five days later, then 10 days later, a month, six weeks and so on.

- Give Value: Make small deposits of value over time to build the relationship and ensure that you only send material the receiver will view as valuable.

  This could be news from your field, bargaining wins, advice, or even invitations to events.

  If you want to know if something is "valuable," ask yourself, "Would someone be disappointed if they missed this email?" If the answer is "no," don't send it.

- Never Break Your Promise: You know the difference between email you want and spam.

  Your messages should be relevant, anticipated and help develop your relationship with the recipient.

  Just because you have someone's email address doesn't give you the right to spam.

Visualize the Result

Imagine you have been engaging workers before they enter the workforce for two years.

Our nursing student now is working at a care home and finds there is no respect or dignity in her workplace.

When you phone and ask how the job is going, she'll already know who you are and that you can help.

Chapter 9: Engaging Union Members in Organizing

The largest resource of industry information and organizing leads is your union's membership.

Union Organizing Referrals and Word of Mouth

Organizing leads that come from members will be stronger than other types of leads because the prospective member knows someone in your union that can speak to his or her personal experience.

What Doesn't Work to Engage Members

One of the more common ways unions have tried to engage members in organizing is to put a notice in the union newsletter that says something like, "If you know anyone who wants to join the union please contact Jason Mann at the union office."

Regrettably, some unions have given up trying to get leads from their members because they got no response to these types of appeals in the union newsletter.

Culture of Organizing

Getting your membership involved in organizing requires a culture of organizing in your union, union staff and members.

Getting staff on board is critical to this process.

If staff members do not buy into the importance of growing the union, how organizing fits into the union, or why it is important to get leads from members, they won't relay the message down to the shop floor.

Disclaimer 1. Without creating a culture of organizing in your union, it is impossible to engage members in organizing in the long term.

Disclaimer 2. These are only tactics to stimulate word of mouth and referrals inside your union, but ultimately it's the actions of your union day to day, and what you achieve for your members, that are the most powerful tools for generating leads from members.

Disclaimer 3. Creating a culture of organizing and getting leads from members isn't something you can fix by Thursday. It requires a long-term, systematic approach.

Can You Have a Goal That is Secret From Your Members?

Although it's something union activists take for granted, members may not be aware your union wants to organize and grow.

They also may not see the impact that organizing and increasing density has on them and their pay.

Regularizing the Organizing Conversation

A discussion about organizing and about getting organizing leads should be part of every meeting in your union because "organizing" isn't a department - it's a job of the union.

If growth is a goal of your union, you can't possibly hope to achieve that goal if you don't tell your members.

Organizing messages need to be built into all of your union's servicing visits and interactions. It's not enough for your rep to ask, "Do you know anyone who wants to join our union?"

Give Reasons

You must provide reasons and demonstrate what new organizing means to existing membership.

Few members will go out and talk about joining a union with their friends as a favour to their servicing rep.

Demonstrate that organizing is building the power of the union, and that with more power you are able to get better contracts and better serve the members you already have.

What's in It for Me?

The reason for a member to get involved in organizing can't be abstract.

It can't just be because it's good for the union or good for society or the right thing to do.

While all of these things are true, you need to get specific on how organizing a new unit benefits existing members.

Elements of Generating Referrals

There are six elements to getting referrals from your members: overcoming barriers, specific asks, repeat referrals, motivation, giving recognition, and timing.

Overcoming Barriers

1. Knowledge of the process:

   Your members may not be providing you referrals because they don't know what the organizing process involves, don't know the union wants to organize or don't know who in the union to refer organizing leads to.

   Your members cannot talk to their friends about joining a union unless they know the answers to these questions.

   The more knowledge your members have, the more confidence they'll have in talking with their friends.

2. What you do with referrals:

   Your members may not provide referrals because they aren't

sure what happens once they give you their friend's contact.

Are you going to show up outside their workplace?
Are you going to put their friend's name in a leaflet?
Are you going to call them?

Members will be hesitant to refer names unless they understand what the union does with the information because your member's reputation is on the line.

Use Specific Asks

You'll get better results from specific questions than you will with, "Hey, do you have any friends that want to join our union?"

Asking, "The union is looking to speak with people who work at Comcast. Do you know anyone who works there?" makes it easier for members to help you.

Look for Repeat Referrals

Members who have provided your union with organizing leads in the past are likely to do it again if you keep them close.

You should call people who have given referrals in the past and look for small ways they can continue to be involved or ways to recognize their accomplishment.

Members who have given you referrals in the past might also make great candidates for a volunteer organizing committee.

Motivating Members to Give Referrals

Recognizing members who give referrals and creating a sense of ownership in the union are the best motivators for getting people to give referrals.

I've worked with unions that have experimented with giving cash in exchange for organizing leads but the tactic rarely works.

Giving members cash for leads ultimately undermines an organizing culture because members are helping for money rather than doing it because it is the right thing to do.

Additionally, it opens up the union for criticism during organizing drives if an employer finds out you paid a member to provide the initial lead.

Saying Thank You

You need to publically thank members who provide you with leads, especially leads that turn into successfully organized units.

It could be in your union newsletter, at a special event for people who have given referrals or by providing union swag or jackets.

Recognition is a powerful motivator.

Instead of a sentence in your newsletter that says, "If anyone knows someone who wants to join a union, call Bob at the union office," put in a story about one of your members who helped one of his friends join your union and emphasize how it all got started because of the member's referral.

By recognizing members, you accomplish two goals: encouraging repeat referrals and demonstrating the type of activity you'd like your members to help with.

The Importance of Timing

Some times are better than others to engage members in organizing.

During contract campaigns it is easier for members can see a link between the current power of the union and the state of negotiations.

It is easier in these situations to point out that organizing means building power, and that a stronger union means better representation and more power at the bargaining table.

Another time to engage members in organizing or run a referral campaign is after you sign a new contract.

Members likely have told their friends their pay increase, and it provides a reason for your members to talk to their friends about the union.

Collecting Testimonials

Collecting testimonials - ideally video testimonials - from your members is another way to get organizing leads from your members.

Not only are testimonials useful for campaign material - asking a member to provide a testimonial is a great opportunity to ask about organizing leads.

Video testimonials are the best response to employers who suggest during an organizing campaign that a union is a third party, separate from its members.

Organizing Wins

Recently organized members are your best potential source of organizing leads.

They can describe to their friends exactly what the organizing process involves and what joining a union has meant to their workplace.

Your organizers already have a relationship with these workers.

Running a referral campaign at a recently organized workplace is a way to transition servicing staff into the workplace.

It can be hard for new members to go from seeing a staff member of the union almost every day during the organizing drive to only occasionally once the unit is certified.

Volunteer Organizing Committees

Setting up a volunteer organizing committee can generate new organizing leads and tap into the knowledge and skills of your members.

Volunteer organizing committees can help with a variety of functions, from doing house calls, worksite visits, phoning, leafleting or meeting to discuss leads.

Keys to Running a Volunteer Organizing Committee

1. Keep them happy: Ask yourself, "What do members of the committee want to learn and what do they want to do?" If you're fulfilling their needs about what they want to learn, contribute and do, the members will be happy and more likely to stick around.

2. Keep them informed: Volunteer organizers want to feel they're a key part of the union and they'll expect a level of ownership.

3. Define tasks and visions: You should give defined tasks and a shared vision of what you want to accomplish so volunteers on your organizing committee have a sense of direction.

   If you are going to ask them to knock on doors, don't just send them out to knock on doors. First, run through what an ideal house call looks like. Discuss how door knocking fits into the broader strategy of the campaign. Let people know how house calls compare to other activities to get cards signed.

   Just because you know why a tactic is important doesn't

mean all members will.

When people can see how their individual contribution makes a difference to the larger goal, they'll have a greater sense of ownership.

4. Learn each member's talents and interests: Volunteers work harder when they are using their greatest talents and abilities.

   If you give people a task that they love, they'll never stop working.

Appendix: A Quick-Start Guide to Getting More Organizing Leads

Here are 67 simple techniques for getting more organizing leads.

1. Have a spot on your union organizing cards for "former employer"

After successfully organizing a worksite, go back to your union cards and ask supporters to put you in contact with workers from their previous job. You will have an instant testimonial and a great third-party introduction from a worker who is familiar with the organizing process.

2. Get organizing leads to chase you, rather than you chasing them

Use an agitation/education campaign rather than cold leafleting. Do something remarkable and get people talking about you.

3. Record your best organizer on video

Is her message better than your lead generation leaflets? Rewrite your materials to sound more like your best organizer.

4. Hold an industry night

Provide valuable information. Keep a sign-in sheet. Be sure to follow up.

5. Keep an email database of card signers from failed campaigns

You know these are people who are willing to join your union. Keep in touch with them regularly. When they find work with another employer – you'll be on the top of their mind.

6. Stop cold leafleting

Cold leafleting is a little like proposing marriage to strangers in a singles bar. It might work, but there are much better ways to accomplish your goal.

7. Keep in touch with your union's former members

Workers who are no longer members of your union don't drop off the face of the earth; they usually stay in the same industry. Print out a list of former members once a month and make calls to see how their new job is going.

8. Install website analytics to your website

Google Analytics gives you measurable information to see how people interact with your website. This is a great tool to measure the effectiveness of outreach activities, ensuring you are not wasting organizing resources.

9. Call your own union and try to join

What obstacles did you face?

What was frustrating?

Eliminate as many barriers as possible between the initial contact with a prospective member and the first meeting.

10. Create a white paper for your website that workers can receive by email

Something like, "Top-Paying Electrical Contractors in San Jose." Keep in touch with this list to pass on valuable information.

11. Learn from best practices

Research to learn what other unions are doing. Phone other organizers. Implement the best ideas.

12. Put up organizing videos for your union on YouTube

Did you know YouTube is the second most popular search engine in the world? There is a trend for web users to do research on YouTube. Be ahead of this trend.

13. Put up posters in your organized worksites

Create a toll-free line for members who want to share an organizing lead.

14. Spend your time empowering members to bring in organizing leads rather than doing all the work yourself

More of an approach than a tip – but it works!

15. Punch the big guy in the face

Select the best-recognized companies in your industry and organize them first. Once you organize the "impossible" you change people's perceptions of what is possible for them (think of the effect organizing Wal-Mart would have on the retail sector).

16. Establish a toll-free organizing hotline for prospective members

Connect it to your cell phone and answer it personally, 24 hours a day. Workers may be wary of leaving a message on a strange voicemail – especially when they feel their job is at risk.

17. Always experiment

No one has a magic formula for organizing. We can't improve by doing what we've always done.

18. Approach members for leads

Your members are the best source for organizing leads if you approach them effectively.

19. Establish a positive campaign around hot-button issues in your industry

Engage non-union workers in the campaign and ensure list building is a critical part of it.

20. Pick strategic targets where you will be able to organize for power

Look for leverage points. Bargaining power = good contracts = more organizing.

21. Build a list of non-union prospects

Conduct a petition aimed at non-union worksites around an issue-based campaign to increase your contact database.

22. Advertise your union (without breaking the bank)

Use Facebook advertising targeted at people who work for a specific employer you are trying to organize.

23. Set up Facebook pages

Facebook is a great tool to generate union organizing leads. But don't spam people.

24. Start a volunteer union organizing committee from your membership

25. Add a live-chat feature to your website

A phone number or contact form is great for workers ready to join immediately. Live chat lets you engage workers in the research stage of joining a union.

26. Ask members for their previous employers when they sign their membership card

You can use this information to build a database of members who have knowledge about your current organizing targets.

Think of the information UFCW would have on Wal-Mart if they asked current members at grocery stores what their last job was.

27. Picture the ideal worker who might contact you

How do your union organizing materials appeal to this person? Picture writing union leaflets to this person and stay focused.

28. Table at community events

29. Better yet . . .

Set up a table at any event where 1,000 people or more will attend, such as sporting events, concerts etc.

30. Connect with academic researchers

Research exists detailing how some unions have turned around their organizing activities to achieve success.

31. Hold classes for your membership on union organizing

It changes the perspective on how your membership thinks about organizing. You might find a great organizer within your membership.

32. Discuss organizing as part of every servicing meeting

33. Use video testimonials

Go through your existing certifications with a video camera - or flip cam - and record video testimonials of your members.

34. End mistakes in communication

Don't make common communications mistakes in your recruitment leaflets such as having a website address that is hard to remember, or expecting materials to look professional without hiring a professional designer.

35. Speak to future workers in their classrooms before they enter the workforce

People are more comfortable learning about the union away from the prying eyes of their employer.

36. Find ways to get contact information of future workers before they enter the workplace

Try helping student societies, holding industry nights or offering a student membership in your union.

37. The best way to get union-organizing leads from students is to go slow

Build a relationship slowly by delivering valuable information.

38. Use Facebook to find employee lists

Most worksites now have Facebook groups or pages for workers to join. If your target doesn't have a Facebook page, create it.

39. Find contact information fast

Take the first name/last name list you made from Facebook and run it against a service such as WhitePages Pro. WhitePages Pro searches several databases to find contact information for your list and you only pay for names it finds.

40. Select the right campaigns

Look for organizing campaigns that can inspire your members and have a direct link to their pocketbook.

41. Build a culture of organizing in your local

Frame organizing in terms of building power for existing members.

42. Set up employee associations as a precursor to union organization

The oldest rule in the union organizer's handbook is to start where the people are. Polls suggest that workers see a big difference between "unions" and "associations."

43. Make your intentions to organize clear to your membership

You can't achieve any goal that is a secret to your membership.

44. Forward leads to other unions – don't underestimate reciprocity

45. Constantly refine your union's join page

Test what works and what doesn't using split testing.

46. Ensure union staff has time to dedicate to getting new organizing leads

Who in your organization is working to make your phone ring?

47. Have an option to "send in an organizing tip" on your website

48. Excite members!

Provide such good servicing that members will want to tell friends about their union.

49. Survey your members

It's inexpensive to conduct a survey by email using a program such as Survey Monkey. Ask questions that will prompt members to express an interest in organizing. Make a list of these folks and follow up with them.

50. Raise expectations in the non-union sector

The labour movement was organized around large ideas that inspired action, including the eight-hour workday, workplace safety, etc. What is the big dream in the industry you are organizing?

51. Try "social brainstorming"

Have a member put his or her name on a piece of paper, along with their current and former jobs. They should then list everyone they know at those workplaces. This is the easiest way to get leads from members who may have forgotten past contacts.

52. Don't chase hot shops

Hot shops are ok if you can get them, but you will never meet your organizing goals if you spend all your time chasing hot shops.

53. Harness the power of social proof in your union leaflets

Remember, you aren't just convincing people to join the union;

you're persuading them to make a phone call. Use testimonials and the principle of social proof, where workers talk about giving you a call.

54. Video testimonials are the most effective form of social proof

55. Cold leaflet the right way

If you must cold leaflet to find leads, use an indirect approach rather than a direct approach. If you use the direct approach (join our union today!) you might leave burnt turf. If you use an indirect approach (you deserve what the union shop down the road gets), the worst-case scenario is that you generate awareness.

56. Ask for less information on your "contact-us form"

The more information you require, the less people will put in the form. It seems simple, but this tactic will get more union leads on your website.

57. Scan your mailbox

Collect every direct mail piece you get in the mail. Look at the formats and headings. You can copy techniques and formulas that work for direct-response marketers, rather than trying to re-invent things yourself.

58. Segment your email marketing lists

Use a service like MailChimp to manage your emails to prospective members. You can check to see who opens your emails over and over. These are good people to call up.

59. Use online advertising

Google Adwords is a great way to communicate messages to relevant workers who are searching for information on how to join a union.

60. Collect leads on your Facebook Page

Set up a tab on your Facebook page to collect email addresses to supplement your email campaigns.

61. Don't lose any information on potential leads

Keep detailed notes in a computerized database or contact management system. Organizers have a high rate of turnover, and information on prospects and leads is often lost when organizers change positions.

62. Recognize members

Recognize and reward members who help organize a workplace or provide an organizing lead. Recognition guarantees repeat referrals.

63. Pay close attention to websites that "rate" former employers

These sites can contain a gold mine of information you can use to create cold leaflets.

64. Focus your time on activities with the highest return

You can easily double your leads by quantifying the effectiveness of each lead-generating tactic. Rank your tactics and focus on the top three activities on the list.

65. Get testimonials and referrals from members who have recently joined your union

Send the testimonials to your prospective member email list.

66. Look for complaints

Pay attention to complaints filed by non-union workers with government ministries. Try to get in contact with them.

67. Think big thoughts and run big campaigns

Small demands and small ideas excite no one. Even if you are unsuccessful in gaining certification, you might inspire future action.

To get free training videos
on four of the best ideas
from this book visit

www.PromotingYourUnion.com